# Christmas Carols For Alto Saxophone With Piano Accompaniment Sheet Music Book 1

Michael Shaw

**Copyright © 2015 Michael Shaw.** All rights reserved. Including the right to reproduce this book or portions thereof, in any form. No part of this text may be reproduced in any form without the express written permission of the author.

**Music Arrangements.** All Christmas Carol arrangements in this book by **Michael Shaw Copyright © 2015**

**ISBN: 1515218015**
**ISBN-13: 978-1515218012**

www.mikesmusicroom.co.uk

# Contents

| | |
|---|---:|
| Introduction | |
| Away In A Manger: Alto Saxophone | 1 |
| Away In A Manger: Alto Saxophone & Piano | 2 |
| While Shepherds Watched: Alto Saxophone | 3 |
| While Shepherds Watched: Alto Saxophone & Piano | 4 |
| The First Noel: Alto Saxophone | 6 |
| The First Noel: Alto Saxophone & Piano | 7 |
| Good King Wenceslas: Alto Saxophone | 9 |
| Good King Wenceslas: Alto Saxophone & Piano | 10 |
| The Holly And The Ivy: Alto Saxophone | 12 |
| The Holly And The Ivy: Alto Saxophone & Piano | 13 |
| Hark The Herald Angels Sing: Alto Saxophone | 15 |
| Hark The Herald Angels Sing: Alto Saxophone & Piano | 16 |
| O Come All Ye Faithful: Alto Saxophone | 18 |
| O Come All Ye Faithful: Alto Saxophone & Piano | 19 |
| We Wish You A Merry Christmas: Alto Saxophone | 21 |
| We Wish You A Merry Christmas: Alto Saxophone & Piano | 22 |
| Silent Night: Alto Saxophone | 24 |
| Silent Night: Alto Saxophone & Piano | 25 |
| Deck The Halls: Alto Saxophone | 27 |
| Deck The Halls: Alto Saxophone & Piano | 28 |
| About The Author | 30 |

# Introduction

The sheet music in this book has been arranged for Alto Saxophone. There are two versions of every piece in this book. The first version is an Alto Saxophone only arrangement, the second version is an Alto Saxophone and piano accompaniment arrangement. Both versions are for beginners and easy to play. The piano parts in this book can be played on a piano, keyboard or organ.

**Versions Of This Book For Other Instruments**

As well as playing duets with piano in this book you can also play together in a duet or ensemble with other instruments with a sheet music book for that instrument.

To get a book for your instrument choose from the Christmas Carols With Piano Accompaniment Book 1 series. Instruments in this series include, Clarinet, Trumpet, Trombone, Tuba, Flute, Tenor Saxophone, French Horn and Alto Saxophone. Please check out my author page on Amazon to view these books.

**Author Page US**
amazon.com/Michael-Shaw/e/B00FNVFJGQ/

**Author Page UK**
amazon.co.uk/Michael-Shaw/e/B00FNVFJGQ/

# Away In A Manger
## Alto Saxophone

Traditional

# Away In A Manger
## Alto Saxophone & Piano

Traditional

# While Shepherds Watched Their Flocks
Alto Saxophone

Traditional

# While Shepherds Watched Their Flocks
## Alto Saxophone & Piano

Traditional

# The First Noel
Alto Saxophone

Traditional

# The First Noel
## Alto Saxophone & Piano

Traditional

# Good King Wenceslas
## Alto Saxophone

Traditional

# Good King Wenceslas
## Alto Saxophone & Piano

Traditional

# The Holly And The Ivy
## Alto Saxophone

Traditional

# The Holly And The Ivy
## Alto Saxophone & Piano

Traditional

# Hark The Herald Angels Sing
## Alto Saxophone

Mendelssohn

# Hark The Herald Angels Sing
## Alto Saxophone & Piano

Mendelssohn

# O Come All Ye Faithful
## Alto Saxophone

John Francis Wade

18

# O Come All Ye Faithful

Alto Saxophone & Piano

John Francis Wade

# We Wish You A Merry Christmas
## Alto Saxophone

Traditional

# We Wish You a Merry Christmas
## Alto Saxophone & Piano

Traditional

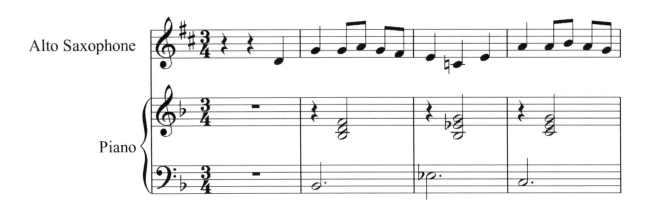

# Silent Night
Alto Saxophone

Traditional

# Silent Night

Alto Saxophone & Piano

Traditional

# Deck The Halls
## Alto Saxophone

Traditional

# Deck The Halls
Alto Saxophone & Piano

Traditional

# About the Author

Mike works as a professional musician and keyboard music teacher. Mike has been teaching piano, electronic keyboard and electric organ for over thirty years and as a keyboard player worked in many night clubs and entertainment venues.

Mike has also branched out in to composing music and has written and recorded many new royalty free tracks which are used worldwide in TV, film and internet media applications. Mike is also proud of the fact that many of his students have gone on to be musicians, composers and teachers in their own right.

You can connect with Mike at:

**Facebook**
facebook.com/keyboardsheetmusic

**Soundcloud**
soundcloud.com/audiomichaeld

**YouTube**
youtube.com/user/pianolessonsguru

I hope this book has helped you with your music, if you have received value from it in any way, then I'd like to ask you for a favour: would you be kind enough to leave a review for this book on Amazon? It'd be greatly appreciated!

Thank You
Michael Shaw

Made in the USA
Monee, IL
18 November 2022